Instructor...
to Acc...

TRANSITIONS

From Reading
To Writing

Barbara Fine Clouse
Youngstown State University

McGraw-Hill, Inc.
New York   St. Louis   San Francisco   Auckland   Bogotá
Caracas   Lisbon   London   Madrid   Mexico City   Milan   Montreal
New Delhi   San Juan   Singapore   Sydney   Tokyo   Toronto

Instructor's Manual to Accompany
TRANSITIONS
From Reading to Writing

ISBN 0-07-011428-5

1 2 3 4 5 6 7 8 9 0 WHT WHT 9 0 9 8 7 6 5 4 3

CONTENTS

The Connection between Reading and Writing

Transitions: From Reading to Writing makes the
connection between reading and writing a number of
ways. Obviously, the readings provide a rich
source of ideas for writing. However, beyond that
is apparatus that identifies rhetorical features
and points of style, usage, and grammar apparent in
each reading and that helps students incorporate those
features into their own writing. In other words,
this apparatus allows for the teaching of certain
rhetorical, stylistic, usage, and grammar points
"incidentally," as they naturally emerge during the
reading selections. Specifically, the apparatus
includes

1. A Workshop after each reading that
identifies and explains the feature apparent
in the essay.

2. A Workshop Activity, which is an
exercise that gives students practice with
the point under consideration.

3. An Idea Generation, Drafting, Revising,
or Editing Activity to help students apply
the point to their own work in progress.

The writing assignments are carefully
constructed to help students make the reading/
writing connection. First, because there is a rich
range of assignments of varying lengths, difficulty
levels, and types (from private journal writing to
public academic writing), students should have no
trouble finding reading-based writing topics that
they feel comfortable with. Second, each chapter
includes one "Forming Connections" assignment with
specific suggestions for generating ideas, so
students who have trouble getting started have the
support they need. Also, each chapter of readings
closes with four assignments based on multiple
readings to give students experience drawing ideas
from and seeing connections between more than one
source. Finally, Chapters 4-12 open with

"Springboards," brief readings to stimulate writing.

Using Peer Groups

Peer groups are becoming a staple of the writing
classroom, and Transitions lends itself
readily to collaborative activities. In fact, many
pre-and post reading activities in the text are
specifically designated as group activities. In
addition, you can incorporate collaborative work in
the following ways.

1. After their first, quick reading of a
selection, students can compare their initial
reactions. A spokesperson can report these to
the rest of the class.

2. Peer groups can work collaboratively to
generate ideas for essays they are writing.

3. The reader response questions in Chapter 3
can be used for peer review of drafts.

4. Groups can work collaboratively to answer
the questions following the readings.

5. Groups can take turns "teaching" readings
to the rest of the class.

6. Each group member can keep a reading journal
in which is recorded reactions to readings. The
journal is shared with other group members, who
write their reactions to the first group member's
reactions. The written responses can be ongoing
to maintain a written dialogue about the readings.

7. Group members can bring questions about essays
they are reading or writing to the group and
members can discuss possible answers.

8. Groups can decide on issues they would like
the instructor to tackle in class. Or they can
select essays they would like the class to read.

9. Each group can publish an anthology of its best writing.

10. Group members can take turns reading essays in the text aloud to each other to get a sense of the rhythm and flow of prose.

11. Group members can write a collaborative essay.

12. Groups can study the vocabulary words together and devise quizzes to test each other.

13. Most of the pre- and post reading activities in the book lend themselves to group work.

Using a Reader Response Form

For instructors who incorporate peer review into their classrooms, use of a reader response form is demonstrated in Chapter 3 in the section that describes a student work in progress. That form is reproduced here in case instructors want to model it for ongoing classroom use. Of course, many instructors will want to modify the form to conform to the characteristics of particular assignments and/or points emphasized in class, and such modification is encouraged.
When you incorporate peer review into your classroom, you need not have students look at all aspects of a draft. Rewarding sessions can come from asking students to react to and make suggestions about just one, or maybe two, features of a draft. Try asking students to respond to just the introduction, or just the word choice, or just the choice of details, and so forth. Often, concentrating attention in this way helps students offer more detailed, considered responses.
While use of the reader response form that appears here is optional, peer review generally goes better when students have some kind of written guidelines for their work, whether these are written on the board or in the form of a handout. In addition, while students can be encouraged to talk to each other about the drafts they are reviewing, they should also be encouraged to write

3

down responses so they stay focused on the task at
hand and so the writer has something to take away
from the review session to refer to during
revising.

Finally, while some research and anecdotal
evidence points to uneven results from peer review,
far more evidence points to positive results. Some
of the reported problems with peer review may stem
from failure to "train" students in how to respond
helpfully. Thus, you may want to explain the
difference between helpful responses ("This is an
interesting point. Can you say more?") and less
than helpful responses ("This is fine"). You may
also want to help students overcome their fear of
offering criticism, by showing them how to do so in
a supportive way.

Sample Reader Response Form

1. What is the thesis idea?

2. Is anything unrelated to the thesis idea?

3. Are any points unproven or unexplained?

4. Is anything unclear?

5. Are the ideas in a logical order?

6. Does the opening create interest?

7. Does the conclusion bring the piece to a
satisfying finish?

8. Is there anything not covered above that you
think should be revised?

9. What do you like best about the piece?

Keeping a Journal

Journals are a natural component of writing
courses, and Transitions includes activities

specifically designated as journal entries. Also, Chapter 1 explains how to use journals as part of the active reading process. In addition, the following can be recorded in journals:

1. Questions about readings or anything going on in class.

2. Writing experiments: a trial draft, an imitation of a writer's style, a "get this off your chest" piece.

3. An imagined dialogue between the writers of two of the text's selections.

4. A poem, short short, or drawing inspired by one of the selections.

5. Relevant articles and cartoons cut from newspapers and magazines.

6. Ideas for future essays.

7. Comments on how the class is going and the student's own progress.

8. Explanations of something that angers or annoys the student.

9. Problems the student is facing and possible solutions.

10. Idea generation material.

11. First drafts and trial runs.

12. Reactions to events in the student's life.

13. A childhood memory evoked by a reading.

14. Things that happen in other classes that relate to something in the readings.

15. Description of the student's current writing process.

16. Reactions to the readings.

17. A discussion of the impact a writer's ideas could have if everyone adopted them.

18. A review of earlier journal entries and an explanation of how the student reacts to them now.

ANSWERS TO "LOOKING CLOSER" QUESTIONS

Chapter 4 How We Interact

p. 41 "Have a Nice Day"

1. One possibility is "Have a nice day" is a harmless expression that shows we care about people.

2. Responses will vary, but many students may find paragraphs 8, 9, and 10 humorous.

3. Middleton uses humor to entertain his reader. Because his subject is not a serious one, a serious treatment is not called for.

4. Adding "Have a nice day" relates the closing to the title and helps the essay come full circle and thereby achieve closure. Also, closing this way illustrates that "Have a nice day" is a useful pleasantry.

5. In paragraph 7, the author explains that it is because the expression is uttered automatically and unthinkingly.

6. The couple laughed perhaps as a release of tension following a traumatic, emotional event. The absurdity triggered the release.

<u>p. 46</u> "Unfair <u>Game</u>"

1. Responses will include something like: It is
    unfair for men to assume that unescorted
    women seek their company and to, therefore,
    press their advances.

2. The anecdotes set up a contrast. The opening story
    shows the way things should <u>not</u> be, and the
    closing story shows the way <u>they</u> <u>should</u> be.

3. The title is a pun on "fair game" and shows that
    unescorted women should not be the target of men's
    advances.

4. He called her a name because she refused to keep
    company with him and because she preferred the company
    of her female companion.

5. A polite "no" is not accepted because of the twisted
    belief that "yes" means "no," so only extreme firmness
    will get the message across.

6. Responses will vary, but many may say that the
    issue is important because the harrassment occurs
    frequently enough to be a drain on women's energies.
    Also, the issue is one of discrimination, which is
    inherently important.

<u>p. 51</u> "So <u>Tsi-fai</u>"

1. The school was run by Catholics; it was strict
    and emphasized Catholic values. The teacher was
    rigid, and little deviation from accepted behavior
    was tolerated. Students were under pressure to
    score well, or they would be denied entrance into
    secondary school.

2. He was pressured to take and pass the Secondary
    School Entrance Exam. He was pressured at home to
    do field and domestic chores, and he probably felt
    pressured because he was his family's "biggest
    hope."

3. His parents were illiterate and therefore
    unable to help him with his school work. Paragraph
    7 suggests his parents were stern, uncompassionate,

and demanding, so he probably felt isolated,
pressured, and perhaps unloved.

4. Responses will vary, but many may think that
the pressure and failure he was experiencing may
have become too much for him.

5. No. Paragraph 18 indicates that social and
economic forces contributed to So Tsi-fai's
failure: "He was poor, undisciplined, and lacked
the training and support to pass his exams."

6. Responses will vary, but perhaps because So
Tsi-fai was a victim of social and economic forces
Liu and her classmates may feel some guilt because
they think they could have done something to help.

7. Hong Kong's education system and social
stratification should be reformed.

p. 57 Jennie's Girl Scout Cookies

1. paragraph 1--"She can't remember" is the first
hint of impairment.

paragraph 2--". . . Where you both are loved and
understood" is the second clue.

2. paragraph 15--"It is better to be charming than
correct."

3. Lyle may mean that being right does not allow
people to abuse, attack, or humiliate each other
and that it is better to give up being right than
to hurt someone in the name of justice.

4. The insensitive behavior of Mrs. X is
contrasted with the caring behavior of everyone
else in the store.

5. The conversation advances the narration and
adds vitality and interest.

6. Responses will vary, but many will appreciate
the irony set up at the end.

1.   The opening anecdotes show the special
attention Walker received because she was
attractive. They also show that part of her
ego was invested in being attractive, in order to
make the effects of the accident on her self-
concept understandable.

2.   Walker's sense of self was linked to her level
of attractiveness. When she felt she was cute, she
felt capable and performed well, but when she felt
unattractive, she did not feel capable and
performed poorly. Also, the move to a new school
may have been a contributing factor.

3.   The white man would not take Walker to the doctor.

4.   Walker embraces and kisses herself as evidence
that she has accepted her disfigurement and hence
herself. She dances with herself because, at last,
she is happy with herself.

5.   She is reassured that her child is not
embarrassed and therefore Walker can heal her
psychic wounds. (She expected her daughter to be
put off and embarrassed by her mother's deformity.)

6.   The poem and her reaction show that her partial
blindness and fear of total blindness helped her see
clearer and appreciate more.

7.   Walker is saying that much of the world values
girls according to their degree of physical beauty
and that the girls themselves tie their level of
self-esteem to how attractive they think they are.

p. 70   "The Truth about Our Little White Lies"

1.   A possibility is "We all tell little white lies."

2.   We tell lies:

     to protect our egos (paragraph 2)
     to escape punishment (paragraph 3)

to avoid disapproval (paragraph 3)
to spare someone's feelings (paragraph 4)
to protect our interests (paragraph 4)

3. Responses will vary.

4. Some readers may think paragraph 3 needs
examples of lies that are social justifications
and that paragraph 4 needs examples of lies that
spare feelings and paragrapj"5 needs examples of
lies oiling the machinery of daily life.

5. Responses will vary.

p. 76 "Just Walk on By: A Black Man Ponders His
Power to Alter Public Space"

1." The opening two sentences lead the reader to
expect a narrative about an act of violence, but
the essay quickly goes on to reverse this
expectation. The irony is clever and effective:
foul play is assumed, as Staples is assumed to be a
threat.

2. A. The thesis is something like: A young black man
is perceived as menacing whether he really is or not;
this perception can be dangerous to the black man.

    B. paragraph 2: "And soon I gathered that
being perceived as dangerous is a hazard in
itself."

3. People who perceive danger, especially if they
are armed, may attack the person they see as a
threat.

4. Women are vulnerable to street violence
(paragraph 6), and young black males are
overrepresented among perpetrators of street
violence (paragraph 6).

5. examples: · paragraphs 3, 9, and 13
    narration: paragraphs 1, 10, and 11

                  contrast: the perception of Staples as a
                               menacing street thug and the gentle,
                               professional man he is

6. A. Their poverty and powerlessness lead them
to it, as does the "male romance with the power to
intimidate.

        B. He saw what happened to thugs and went in
the opposite direction: he became a "shadow" for
fear of ending badly.

               Chapter 5 Youth and Age

p. 84 "Old at Seventeen"

1. paragraph 2, sentence 1: "The most major
signal up to now that I was getting old happened
late last winter when Richie and Micah appeared at
my front door early in the morning."

2. The author does not want to sled down the hill
because he is afraid. This information is made
clear in the conclusion. Responses to the rest
of the questions will vary.

3. paragraph 4: Vecsey wore boots instead of
sneakers.
        paragraph 5: Old Glory seemed smaller.
        paragraph 11: Vecsey would rather play
negotiation than hijack the sled.
        paragraph 13: Vecsey is no longer weatherproof
        paragraph 13: Vecsey would rather watch TV or
read than sled.
        paragraph 14: Now Vecsey knows fear; he did
not when he was younger.

        The contrasts heighten the differences between
the seventeen-year-old Vecsey and the boy, thus
establishing that he has matured beyond some
childhood activities.

4. Paragraphs 3, 5, 6, 7, 9, 10, 11, and 12
include humor and exaggeration. The humor and
exaggeration add a light-hearted tone that lets the
reader know the author doesn't really consider

himself old. Also, they help make the essay
enjoyable.

5. Most readers will think paragraph 14 makes the
most serious point: As we age, fear assumes a
larger role in our lives.

6. Responses will vary.

p. 90 "My Grandmother, the Bag Lady"

1. Possessions represented security and a measure
of control over her life. They were also all she
had left. (Refer to paragraph 14.)

2. She still can make choices (she chose not to
wake up anyone, for example), and she controls the
possessions she has left by keeping them in a bag.

3. The woman has dignity, courage, and a degree of
independence in that she exercises free choice.
She is a survivor.

4. Neal uses descriptive language to move the
reader's emotions. For example, in paragraph 12,
her grandmother's space "diminished like melting
butter." Desccriptions like this and the ones
in paragraphs 8, 14, and 18 evoke pathos and
sympathy.

5. The repetition emphasizes the grandmother's
diminishing space.

6. Many readers will find the conclusion
satisfying because it is emotional and powerful.

p. 96 "Complexion"

1. Rodriguez was self-conscious about his
complexion, believing he was too dark to a be
attractive to girls. He felt shame and sexual
inferiority.

12

2. The women in his family contributed to his feelings.

3. Rodriguez's mother made him feel that dark skin was unattractive to women when she told him to cover his shoulders just after she had been sexually admiring Rodriguez's lighter-skinned father. His aunts made him feel undesirable when they discussed ways to lighten dark skin.

4. Rodriguez felt too ugly to date, so he read about sex and romance. He tried to shave off his darkness. He denied himself simple pleasures like biking with his shirt off. He avoided participation in physical education classes.

5. Rodriguez read partly as a substitute for the experiences he was not having because he felt ugly. He was afraid the reading would make him effeminate because reading, like other forms of education, was not a "manly, physical" activity.

6. Responses will vary.

p. 101 "Aging in the Land of the Young"

1. No, Curtain is not bigoted against old people. The last paragraph is an affirmation of the value of the elderly.

2. The mothers have more years of cultural conditioning, so they are more bigoted against the elderly. Also, they are more aware of their own mortality, and thus they are more likely to fear the aged.

3. The description moves the reader's emotions and provides strong mental images.

4. Paragraphs 16 and 17 include examples that help establish the fear of the elderly and how we shun them.

5. the last paragraph: We are losing the sense of history and identity the elderly would provide if we did not shun them.

6. Curtin's purpose is to persuade the reader to cast off any prejudice against the elderly. Her audience is the young and the middle-aged.

p. 107 "Kids in the Mall: Growing Up Controlled"

1. The last sentence of paragraph 4 could be said to form the thesis.

2. Because the examples are dramatic, they arouse interest. They also show how serious the problem is, since the next paragraph says the stories are not unusual.

3. paragraphs 7, 10, 11, 13, 14, 15, and 16

4. Kowinski believes that kids are harmed by the mall.
   paragraph 9: The mall teaches materialism.
   paragraph 12: The mall "encourages passivity and consumption."
   paragraph 13: Kids who work in the mall have no real career goals.
   paragraph 14: Kids who work in the mall work with other teens.

5. Kowinski does not have much faith in the educational benefits of malls. Not many benefits are noted, and those that are get so little development that the author must not find them very compelling.

6. Responses will vary.

p. 112 "And Maybe I Can Also Walk on Water"

1. Cosby is pointing out the relativity of age: "Old age" comes later, the older we become. He is also playing for its entertainment value an inevitable fact of life: the aging process. Despite the serious point, Cosby's purpose is probably to entertain his reader.

2.   The title is apt; it suggests that holding aging
and death at bay would be just as much of a miracle
as walking on water. In other words, it says that
we will all age and die--which is the point of the
essay.

3.   Responses will vary.

4.   Children know that people die, but they never
think death will happen to them. They think of
themselves as living forever, while death comes to
those they perceive as "old"--advanced age being a
state they never expect to reach.

5.   Cosby contrasts how he feels about aging and
dying from the perspective of a fifty-year-old and
how he felt about them as a child. He also contrasts
being "old" with feeling young.

6.   Yes, because Cosby writes about feeling younger
than his years.

p. 117 "Our Youth Should Serve"

1.   The last sentence of paragraph 3 expresses the
thesis idea.

2.   Muller wants to persuade the reader that
mandatory volunteer service for teenagers is a good
idea.

3.   The description begins with the thesis--the last
sentence of paragraph 3

4.   Objections are treated in paragraphs 5, 6, and 10.

5.   Youth would feel useful.
     Society would be served.
     Graduates would get job training.
     Graduates would get pay toward post-service
     education.
     Graduates would be more highly motivated.
     Graduates might locate careers.

6.   Responses will vary.

"They Shut My Grandmother's Room Door"

1. In America, people often die alone, but in Vietnam, people die "in their homes surrounded by neighbors and relatives" (paragraph 4).

2. A. Americans fear death and, therefore, we isolate our elderly in convalescent homes so we don't have to watch death and its approach. The Vietnamese accept death--they even "used to stare death in the face" (paragraph 7), so they don't isolate their elderly.

   B. Lam prefers the Vietnamese approach.

3. The closed door symbolizes hiding death away (behind the closed door), so we can keep it hidden, and thus we don't have to deal with it as directly.

4. The point is that the Vietnamese way of dealing with death provides unity and coherence--a "connection" between life and death. In the American "disjointed" way, death is disconnected from life because we isolate the elderly from mainstream living.

5. A. The description adds vividness and emotional impact.

   B. Examples appear in paragraph 9. They add poignancy and help prove the point that Americans cannot escape the reality of suffering in old age.

6. Responses will vary, but many may think that the contrast shows a better alternative to the American way. The contrast helps establish the error of the American way.

Chapter 6 Family

p. 129 "Growing Up with Trux"

1. They shared a love of sports; they moved often so the author depended on his father for entertainment; and the author was an only child.

2. The separation may have been inevitable because of the natural pulling away that occurs during adolescence.

3. It is a natural and normal part of maturation to reconcile with parents after the equally natural split that occurs with adolescence and young adulthood.

4. He wrote to share his feelings for his father and perhaps to pay him tribute

5. Yes. The fact that the author and his father were bound by a love of sports makes the essay well suited to readers of Sports Illustrated.

6. Responses will vary.

7. Many readers will appreciate the conclusion because it is emotional and powerful. It leaves the reader with a sense of closure and a sense of the author's love for his father.

p. 135 "No Turning Back"

1. A. Qoyawayma poses a threat to the Hopi culture because she has abandoned traditional Indian beliefs for white religion and white education. Qoyawayma, however, has adopted Christianity and is committed to her new beliefs. She feels a return to Hopi ways would be a step backward.

   B. Qoyawayma has worked hard to forge what she considers to be a better life for herself, and she resists and resents her uncle's demands that she give up her new life.

17

2.   A.   Use of lashed sets up the comparison of the
ritual whipping and Qoyawayma leaving the village
for the white world: both are rites of passage.

     B.   Use of smarting refers to both the pain of
the whipping and the pain of defying her uncle.

3.   The whipping was a rite of passage into a more
mature time of increased knowledge, perhaps about
tribal life and life in general. In other words,
the whipping marked a coming of age.

4.   The idea is that "as you give, so shall you
get," which is one concept of justice.

5.   She felt a conflict of identity: she was
neither true Hopi nor true anything else. Yet the
Hopi ways were with her as she set out to wash her
hair, showing that she hadn't completely severed
the connection (and never would) to her heritage.

6.   The rite of passage was to open the door to
wisdom--perhaps Qoyawayma felt that acquiring
Christianity amounted to that very thing. Also,
paragraph 7 notes that the stinging of her uncle's
words reminded her of the sting of the lash.

7.   Leaving one culture for another is painful and
(as the last paragraph shows) one never fully casts
off the old ways.

p. 141   "They Stole Our Childhood"

1.   Paragraph 13--"Divorce didn't just split up
parents. It stole our childhood."

2.   The effects include:
     early sexual activity
     overachieving in school
     having adult worries
     spending more time at school and work
     feeling like they've already married and raised
        kids--acting like parents
     pressure to take sides in divorce proceedings
     missed chance to be childish

18

3.   because they hunger for affection
     because having sex means acting like an adult
     because they need a "physical affirmation of
         self-worth" (paragraph 7)

4.   They lose and miss closeness with their
             children.
     They have no memories of their children's
             childhood.
     They are separated from their children and
             don't know why.
     They don't know their children.

5.   The title is effective because it refers to the
main point of the essay. It refers to the fact
that divorced parents rob their children of their
youth by expecting them to assume adult
responsibilities.

6.   Responses will vary.

p. 145 "Letter to My Mother"

1.   The piece has the lyrical quality of a poem.

2.   The child's mastery of English represents the
family's assimilation; it is a sign that
eventually, many of the old ways will be lost,
a fact that is a source of sadness.

3.   Responses will vary, but something like: We
want to live in our own country. Whether good or
bad, it is ours and where we belong.

4.   She stayed behind, sacrificing herself so the
others could make a faster, safer escape from
Vietnam.

5.   This is an apparent reference to lack of
religious freedom.

6.   Responses will vary.

7.   The postal service is unreliable.(para. 1).
     Women don't drive cars (para. 4).

There are no (or few) ice cream stands
    (para. 5).
There is hunger (para. 7).
There is poverty (para. 7).
There is religious repression (para. 14).

p. 150 "An Older Brother Lets Go"

1. Responses will vary, but Marcus was loving and
caring. He was someone who could be counted on for
help and support. He took his older brother role
seriously and always tried to "be there" for his
younger brother.

2. The introduction provides background
information. Many readers will find there is a
dramatic, poignant quality to the introduction that
engages the reader's interest.

3. The anecdotes help the reader see the closeness
between the two brothers.

4. A. Contrast appears in paragraphs 6, 9, 12,
and 13.

    B. Examples appear in paragraphs 3 and 5.

5. Responses will vary.

6. The conclusion includes the last event in the
narration. The author also harkens back to
paragraph 10 by saying the hug is his report card.
The conclusion is effective because it is moving,
and it provides closure.

p. 155 "Hold the Mayonnaise"

1. Mayonnaise represents all that is unfamiliar
and distasteful in American culture. That she
eventually tolerates it in her home is a mark of
Alvarez's greater comfort with American culture.

2. The day was full of confusion because the
family was being redefined and a woman from a

different culture was marrying into the family.
Also, by definition, weddings are usually confusing
in their hecticness. The effort refers to the
energy everyone put into dealing with the
confusion and into keeping things running smoothly.

3. She was uncomfortable being alone with her step
children because she felt like a "newcomer in
someone else's territory."

4. Partly to explain the disparity between her
appearance and theirs and partly because she didn't
feel that she and they had quite bonded, and she
didn't want to presume.

5. Responses will vary, but something like: Take
care of your responsibilities with a loving heart,
and the family members will come to accept each
other.

6. Responses will vary, but many will find that the
conclusion is clever and that the reference to
mayonnaise provides closure.

p. 164 "Our Son Mark"

1. Responses will vary, but most will probably say
that Mark is happy; he has "a capacity for
contentment" and "his world . . . is a happy and
bright one" (paragraph 5).

2. Responses will vary, but many will say no
because Mark has contributed so many positive
things to the family.

3. Responses will vary, but many may feel that we
become embarrassed and awkward around people with
handicaps and as a result we say and do the wrong
things.

4. They had increased understanding of their
children, greater patience, and less of a tendency

to expect too much. They were better able to
accept their children for what they are (paragraph
39).

5. Responses will vary but may include long-term
care, financial support, housing, nurturing,
emotional security, and physical well-being.

6. Hayakawa is sharing and informing his readers
of the joy he and his family experienced by keeping
Mark at home. He is also persuading his readers
that institutionalization is not necessarily the
only or best course of action for the mentally
retarded.

7. Hayakawa is referring to the fact that, as he
is, Mark has had a positive impact on the family.

Chapter 7 Men and Women

p. 172 "Why I Want a Wife"

1. Background information is provided.

2. The categories are:
    financial support and child care (para. 3)
    housekeeping and cooking (para. 4)
    listener (para. 5)
    social director (para. 6)
    lover (para. 7)

3. Brady scorns the role as oppressive and unfair.

4. The audience would be feminists, mostly female.
They are likely to be sympathetic to Brady's
purpose (attacking society's attitude toward the
wifely role) because they want to cast off
traditional roles and achieve equality between the
sexes.

5. A. Men are exploitive, demanding, and
domineering.

B. She is probably not fair; she exaggerates to make a point.

6. The repetition of "I want" emphasizes the selfishness and childishness of anyone who "wants" the stereotypical wife described in the essay.

p. 176 "Blasting Some Unmanly Myths"

1. (She) describes the myth of the stereotpyical man who cannot be controlled or held accountable for his actions no matter how wrong they are because the man can't help himself--he is just like a "force of nature."

She also describes the myth that men are the most rational of beings and in control of everything, including themselves; they are never emotional.

2. The stereotype is described in paragraph 7--the woman is irrational, emotional, and governed by hormones.

3. Responses will vary, but many may find that the brevity and colloquialism of the first sentence of paragraph 10 provide impact which emphasizes the contrast to the stereotype about to be discussed. They may also find that the last sentence of paragraph 11 is, like the introduction, an example of irony. It reinforces the thesis idea: a man can help himself.

4. He does so because it is demeaning; it treats men like boys.

5. The thesis appears in the conclusion: Men do control their own actions, and to say otherwise is to treat men like boys.

6. His audience is likely the average, general reader. (The article first appeared in the Washington Post.) The purpose is likely to inform readers of the myths about males and, therefore, to persuade the audience to reject the male stereotype.

23

p. 183 "India: A Widow's Devastating Choice"

1. A. Anjali killed herself because she was
destitute, and, to her, death was preferable to
abject poverty.

    B. The Indian system being what it is, she may
not have had a viable alternative. Responses,
however, will vary.

2. Suicide is not considered to be the sin
Westerners often think it to be. In fact, at one
time it was considered a cultural, religious, and
economic imperative for widows. Even today, some
think that it has a "social and economic relevance"
for widows.

3. A defense of Anjali's action is probably more
possible in the Indian/Bengali scheme of things
than in the Western Judeo-Christian scheme.

4. A. Anjali's family was upset because she
violated their expectations by finding her own
husband rather than waiting for an arranged match.
Also, Rajib was from a lower caste.

    B. Rajib's family was upset because marrying
out of his caste denied them a significant dowry.

5. Responses will vary, but Anjali's family,
Rajib's family, India's social system, and Anjali
herself all probably share some of the blame.

6. To show that India has a serious problem to
address--the same one Anjali faced. That is,
widows are "superfluous" and have trouble living in
India.

7. Responses will vary, but many will say that the
opening paragraph arouses interest because it is so
dramatic and arresting.

p. 188 "Male Humor"

1. A. The audience is males.

B. The introduction says, "Most of us, if we are male." Also, women are repeatedly referred to as "they" and men as "we."

2. People tell off-color jokes because it is a relief to admit that sex and elimination (the subjects of off-color jokes) exist and because they are funny. (paragraph 9)

3. Asimov may be exaggerating for effect, but he repeats the idea in paragraph 15 and seems serious.

4. Women may be offended because Asimov accuses them of tyrannizing men (paragraphs 12 and 13); he says women can't remember and tell jokes (paragraph 18); he implies women remember only trivial things (paragraph 21); he says that women are responsible for men telling chauvinistic jokes.

5. Rhetorical questions are in paragraphs 3, 10, 11, 16, and 20.

6. The thesis is something like: Men tell chauvinistic, off-color jokes as a release from the domination by women and because women encourage them by not joining in. Therefore, women are responsible for male humor.

p. 194   "Notes at Midterm: The Quintessential Mom Goes Back to School"

1. Before: Heilman felt insecure and full of self-doubt; she saw herself as a "throw-back to the distant past--the quintessential mom."

   After: Heilman felt confident that she "could rally to get the job done"; she was looking ahead to a job after graduation.

2. That she was the product of an earlier era, when women gave up careers and education to marry and raise children.

3. Paragraph 9 explains how hectic it can get trying to juggle multiple roles, and it explains that the wife-mother-student sometimes needs help.

25

Paragraph 10 describes some of the awkwardness
the middle-aged wife-mother can feel as a student.

4. Her advice is "go for it; you can do it; just
have faith in yourself and be willing to work hard."

5. Her audience is older, retired people.
    Her purpose is to let the reader know middle-aged
    women can return to school and succeed; perhaps
    one purpose is to inspire older women

6. Many readers are likely to say yes for two
reasons: the reference to school, which students
can relate to, and the reference to throwing up,
which is an attention-getter.

p. 199 "Television Insults Men, Too"

1. The thesis is that it is considered acceptable
to ridicule males on television. This thesis is
best expressed in paragraph 3.

2. Three examples of insulting commercials are
given, but only one example of an insulting program
is given--although the example is of a hit show.

3. Responses will vary, but some may feel the need
for additional examples of insulting programs.

4. It is generally agreed that racism on
television is completly inappropriate, so by
raising the racist image associated with Stepin
Fetchit, Goldberg makes male gender bias seem
equally unacceptable. In paragraph 12, Goldberg
uses the same kind of associative logic when he
compares the female to a male batterer.

5. Since paragraph 14 treats the print medium,
it's not strictly relevant. It does, however,
provide the transition to paragraph 15, where all
media are mentioned.

6. The audience is the average, general reader.
The purpose is to inform readers that an
injustice against men exists and to persuade
readers to share this view.

Chapter 8 Bias and Discrimination

p. 209 "Don't Just Stand There"

1. "Left unchecked, racial slurs and
offensive ethnic jokes 'can poison the atmosphere'"
(paragraph 4), and speaking up makes it more likely
that a person's behavior will change--especially if
enough people speak up (paragraph 5). Also,
speaking up makes us feel better about ourselves
(paragraph 7).

2. A. Momentary satisfaction is offset by
lowering yourself and by the risk of being labeled
thin-skinned or someone not to be taken seriously.
Also, the situation could escalate to new insults
or violence.

   B. A private talk with the person who told the
joke, in which you explain how the joke made you
feel.

3. He or she will deny the offense to save face.
If the person meant no offense, an unnecessary rift
will occur.

4. If kids learn how to handle ethnic
slurs, they will be able to do so as adults. Also,
kids encounter ethnic slurs all the time and may
have difficulty dealing with them because of peer
pressure. Finally, children are the hope for a
better, less-biased future.

5. A. something like: When one hears a racist
remark, ethnic slur, or any insulting remark about
a person's background, he or she should take
action.

   B. The title relates to the thesis because it
is an admonishment to take action.

6. The examples serve to clarify points so the
reader better understands them.

<u>p.</u> <u>213</u>   "<u>Black</u> <u>and</u> <u>Latino</u>"

1.   Santiago uses an interestng quotation.

2.   The thesis is expressed in paragraph 1, the last
2 sentences.

3.   The conflict is that he has two heritages, and
people expect him to choose one and deny the other.
He resolves the conflict by refusing to do that--he
embraces both his black and Latino heritages.

4.   Puerto Ricans are not taught black-white racism
as they are growing up, but people in the United
States are "raised with that hang-up" (paragraph 9).

5.   Whites express bias towards him because he
appears to be black, and blacks are not always
accepting because he does not act black.

6.   Paragraph 7 includes an anecdote that
illustrates that Santiago has been a victim of
discrimination because of his black skin.

<u>p.</u> <u>218</u>   "<u>It</u> <u>Is</u> <u>Time</u> <u>to</u> <u>Stop</u> <u>Playing</u> <u>Indians</u>"

1.   Many readers may feel that the first sentence
effectively stimulates interest by arousing
curiosity; the reader wants to read on to discover
what "it" is.

2.   paragraph 3

3.   paragraphs 1, 2, 6, and 8

4.   Hirschfelder means that in schools, units and
plays hide the truth about Indians because they
perpetuate the stereotype. The use of <u>mask</u> is
interesting because it harkens to Halloween masks
worn by children in Indian costumes--a reference to
paragraph 1.

5. Native Americans are offended (para. 3).
We fail to understand authentic Indian
culture (para. 3).
Indians are prevented from being "a relevant
part of the nation's social fabric"
(para. 3).
History is masked (para. 4).
Real people are disguised (para. 6).
Indian children get negative information about
their heritage (para. 7).
Indians are denigrated (para. 7).

6. By offering Indian dress, icons, and symbols as
playthings (paragraph 6).

p. 222 "Excess Baggage Is Not a Firing Offense"

1. paragraph 2, sentence 1

2. A. The examples are word play because they are
references to overweight.

B. In her last sentence, Sachs says "tip the
scales."

3. Some readers may find the word play clever, and
some may feel that it detracts from the seriousness
of the issue.

4. She means that American Airlines did not fire
Cappello because she could not do the work but
because she did not conform to their standards of
attractiveness.

5. She provides background information.

6. She looks to the future.

p. 227 "Don't Let Them See You Cry"

1. Responses will vary, but many readers are
likely to find the opening image dramatic and
compelling.

29

2. Much about integrating Central High was warlike: troops were called in, some violence occurred, the potential for death existed, new ground was secured, and the nine had to fight every day for the political and moral ideal of integration.

3. If the white mob saw her cry, they would take it as a sign of weakness, as a sign that they were winning. Elizabeth couldn't give them that power.

4. They want to show the success of the civil rights movement.

5. The idea was to reduce the likelihood of violence.

6. Responses will vary.

p. 231 "An Act of Conscience"

1. Responses will vary, but one possibility is that the club was so important to his career and therefore the well-being of his family that he may have "looked the other way."

2. When Henry Bloch, who is Jewish, was denied admission, the restrictive policies struck too close to Watson's home.

3. A. Garrity is opposed to restrictive admission policies and in favor of what Watson did.

    B. paragraph 1: "I almost cheered when I read Friday morning's front-page headline in The Kansas City Star . . . ."

    paragraph 5: "Those of us who knew Watson and the Kansas City Country Club have long wondered how he handled the competing loyalties of club and family."

    paragraphs 6, 9, 10, 13, 14

4. The reference is to the hoods worn by members of the Klu Klux Klan.

5.   They are afraid of incurring the disapproval of their peers and afraid of suffering financially because of reprisals taken against them in the business world.

6.   Garrity closes by looking to the future.

p. 238   "Nora Quealey"

1.   She needed the money.

2.   poverty
     lack of education
     exploitation of workers
     her sense of responsibility to her children

3.   Paragraphs 8, 9, 10, and 11 show that the company has little regard for its employees and exploits them.

4.   sex discrimination (paragraphs 4, 5, 13)
     racial discrimination (paragraph 10)
     exploitation of workers (paragraphs 8, 9, 11, and 12)

5.   Poverty means that Quealey must put up with all the discrimination that comes her way because she cannot afford to quit her job and escape the discrimination.

6.   Responses will vary, but students should come to appreciate the difficulty (if not the futility) of Quealey's situation.

Chapter Nine   Education

p. 247   "Life Is Not Measured by Grade-Point Averages"

1.   something like: Students are too concerned with grades and the jobs that education leads to.

31

Instead, they should be interested in seeking knowledge.

2. The story illustrates Miller's point that students are more concerned with getting an education so they can get a job than with acquiring knowledge for its own sake.

3. Universities used to be finishing schools and country clubs for the wealthy or places to prepare for careers in the clergy or teaching; now we see universities as places where job training is provided. Today grades and job training are more important than the goal of knowledge acquisition, the goal in the past.

4. Miller says that students worry too much about money, which is overrated. He believes "it's not lack of money but the fear of the lack of money" that is a problem--yet students need not fear because they will not starve.

5. A. His target audience was those entering college and graduate school.

   B. Responses will vary, but many may believe that Miller's message will fall on deaf ears since many students are probably committed to "job training."

6. Paragraphs 8 and 9 have the quality of speech because you is the understood subject of the verbs, which creates the sense of the reader being spoken to directly.

p. 252 "The Physical Miseducation of a Former Fat Boy"

1. Crew has contempt for physical education teachers because he thinks they care only about the capable students, and they contribute to the poor self-concept of the less capable. He believes they fail to do their jobs because they do not help the less capable.

2. They should have shown him the joys of physical education as a celebration of the body.

3. The last three sentences of paragraph 10 present the thesis.

4. Crew is referring to the stereotype of the jolly fat man who really doesn't mind being overweight and hence can laugh at jokes about his size.

5. Crew feels that competition among people is not always required or desirable. An individual can take joy in personal accomplishments.

6. He became water boy and trainer (para. 7).
   He made friends with athletes (para. 5).
   He worked harder at his books (para 1).

7. The anecdote shows that it is common to equate manhood with a certain level of athletic ability.

p. 259 "Reading for Success"

1. A. At first, Rodriguez got little pleasure from reading. He saw no connection between reading and learning, and he found reading a difficult, slow-going, isolating process.

   B. Rodriguez probably felt the way he did because English was not his first language.

2. He realized that books could educate him, and with education would come success. Thus, his desire to succeed motivated Rodriguez.

3. Reading theory now tells us that there is no single, correct meaning that rests in the text for the reader to discover. Each reader, instead, creates his or her own meaning.

4. Our education system fosters the notion that anything pleasureable is frivolous.

5. Reading gave him pleasure.
   Reading gave him academic success.
   Reading helped him become a confident speaker
       and writer.
   Reading gave him an understanding of Western
       thought.

6. A. Rodriguez felt he was not a good reader
because he had the immature notion that he read to
"acquire knowledge." He tried merely to extract
knowledge; he brought nothing to the text.

   B. Those who subscribe to current reading
theory are likely to agree with Rodriguez.

p. 265   "In an Assault on Tradition, More Schools
            Last All Year"

1. For
       A. Children retain information better.
       B. The year-round calendar is a step
          toward lengthening the school year.
       C. The year-round calendar conforms to
          children's learning patterns.
       D. We no longer need summers off to
          work on the farms.

       E. The current calendar necessitates
          too much review.
       F. The year-round calendar is better for
          students with problems.
       G. Buildings can be used all year.
       H. The year-round calendar keeps urban
          teens in high crime areas off the
          streets.
       I. Teachers don't object to year-round
          calendars.

   Against
       A. Summer vacation is embedded in American
          culture.
       B. Some parents can't adjust to the
          schedule.

34

C. The summer recreational industry is adversely affected.
D. The schedule creates problems when family members are on different schedules.

2. Kirst suggests that no research has yet proven the benefits of year-round schools, so we don't know for sure that the year-round calendar is the better way.

3. Since the beginning of public education in this country, students have had summers off, so the tradition is historical. It is also cultural because parents, teachers, and children have sets of expected behavior patterns that are habitually associated with summer.

4. In our earlier agrarian society, the children were needed to work in the fields.

5. Although pros and cons are given, there is more discussion of pros, so the article seems tipped in favor of year-round schools.

6. Yes, the light-hearted anecdote provides an effective counterpoint to the serious discussion. Also, the paragraphs suggest that the children aren't unduly bothered by the year-round calendar, so it can't be that bad.

p. 270   "Learning to Write"

1. Responses will vary, but some may say that Mr. Flegle didn't really inspire Baker; his lucky choice of a writing topic did.

2. He discovered a motivation: he wanted to write it for his own joy, not for his teacher's ends.

3. Help students to write about topics that matter to them, and they will be motivated (paragraph 7).

Reward performance (ie by reading student work aloud) (paragraph 10).

Try not to let the "rules of formal composition" interfere with writing (paragraph 7).

4. He learned what he wanted to do with his life. He learned that good writing is not goverened by the rules of formal composition.

5. The details are arranged in a chronological order, which is suitable for narration.

6. Baker may have written the essay to share something about his life, and to inform a bit about the nature of education.

p. 275 "Shame"

1. Paragraph 3 explains that the point of the narration is that what happened in the classroom taught him shame and so affected him that he was motivated to excel to overcome that shame.

2. Helene represented everthing that Gregory wanted but did not have.

3. He brushed his hair.
He got a handkerchief.
He washed his clothes in cold water.
He shoveled her walk.
He made friends with her family.
He dropped money on her stoop.
He invented a father for himself.
He announced a contribution to the Community Chest.

4. The sentences are dramatic and attention-getting to stimulate the reader's interest, so students are likely to say that the lines made them want to read on.

5. A. paragraph 4

B.   Paragraphs 1-3 provide background
information that places the story in the
appropriate context.

6.   The conversation adds vitality and interest,
and it advances the narration.

7.   The fragments add a choppiness that adds to the
emotional intensity of the paragraph.

p. 283   "The Lesson"

1.   Miss Moore teaches the children that there is a
tremendous disparity between the rich and the poor
and that the unequal distribution of wealth is an
injustice.

2.   Miss Moore has been to college, and hence she
has been outside the community of her students.
This makes her aware of the world, its workings,
and its injustices.

3.   Perhaps she felt the kids were too sheltered
and needed to know the truth about how the world
operated so they would be motivated to do something
about it.

4.   Several factors may have influenced the reaction:
   A. Miss Moore dressed, spoke, and acted
differently.
   B. She taught the kids when they would rather
have been playing.
   C.   She taught the children a difficult lesson.
   D.   She was a reminder of all they didn't have.

5.   Perhaps Sylvia feels the same awe, respect, and
lack of familiarity for both.

6.   Perhaps Sylvia is so angered and motivated by
the lesson in inequality that she learned that she
vowed never to come up on the "short end of the
equality stick."

7.   Responses will vary.

Chapter Ten   Television

<u>p.</u> <u>291</u> "<u>TV</u> Addiction"

1.   Something like: Some heavy viewers are TV
addicts who suffer damaging effects because of
their addiction.

2.   The quotation functions to support the
statement made in the previous paragraph that TV
addicts watch instead of engaging in other
activities.

3.   The source of this quotation shows that TV
addicts can even come from the ranks of the
educated. Therefore, the addiction has the
potential to affect anyone.

4.   The addict searches for a high that normal
     life doesn't supply (para. 3).

     The addict has an inability to function
     without the addictive substance.(para 3).

     The addictive substance must be experienced
     repeatedly (para. 4).

     The addiction has destructive elements
     (para. 5).

5.   Winn includes the definitions to better draw
the parallel between heavy TV viewers and people
addicted to drugs and alcohol, so the reader sees
similarities and is convinced that TV addiction
does exist and is serious.

6.   Responses will vary.

<u>p.</u> <u>296</u>   "<u>Is</u> <u>TV</u> <u>Ruining</u> <u>Our</u> Children?"

1.   paragraph 4, last sentence: "What is all that
TV viewing doing to kids, and what can be done
about it?"

38

2. A. paragraphs 6, 7, 8, and 12

    B. paragraphs 9 and 10

3. Zoglin provides far more on the negative effects.

4. It is more likely that Zoglin cites authorities to provide an overview of the chief schools of thought on the effects of televison on children.

5. The pervasive impact of television will not be eliminated, but steps can be taken to lesson the negative impact.

6. Parents should exercise control to make sure that there are "counterbalancing influences" in their children's lives.

p. 302   "Don't Blame TV"

1. A. something like: TV is unfairly blamed for many of society's problems.

    B. paragraph 9, the last sentence

2. Yes, the quotation arouses interest and establishes the context for Greenfield's argument: what we claim to know (television is responsible for many social ills) just is not true.

3. decline in SAT scores
    rise in the crime rate
    decline in voter turnout
    increase in the divorce rate
    increase in premarital and
        extramarital sex
    collapse of family life

4. paragraph 6

5. The admission shows that he is aware that television isn't perfect. This makes him seem

more reasonable, so the reader is more likely to believe him.

6.   Responses will vary.

7.   Some readers may find that the references are confusing and that they date the essay. Others may feel that the references do not detract from the validity of the point.

p. 309 "MTV's Message"

1.   something like: We do not know for sure whether the effects of MTV are harmful or not.

2.   for
    The very young aren't harmed because they
        don't understand what they see.
    Other programs are more harmful to the young.
    A study shows no harmful effects on kids.
    The videos are tame and getting tamer.
    Some videos have positive messages.
    Parents can control children's exposure
        to MTV.

    against
    Viewers are made to feel something is wrong
        if they are not sexually active.
    The videos can cause nightmares.
    The dress is inappropriate.
    The videos frighten the very young.
    The videos contain gratuitous violence.

3.   paragraphs 4, 5, 6, and 12

4.   The direct quotations present the opposing sides in an authoritative way and show that authorities disagree on whether or not MTV is harmful.

5.   Responses will vary.

6.   Responses will vary.

40

<u>p.</u> <u>314</u>   "'<u>Live, from San Quentin</u> . . .'"

1.   Many readers are likely to say yes because the
paragraph is dramatic, and the description has
power.

2.   <u>for</u>
          Since the press can cover the execution, TV
               should be able to as well.
          Public executions occur in other countries.
          Public executions occurred in the U.S. in
               the past.
          The identity of the officials involved can
               be electronically masked.
          Taste is not an issue.
        - Some abolitionists say that public executions
               will convince people to do away with the
               death penalty.

     <u>against</u>
          Televising executions would be brutalizing.
          Empathy will be created for the condemned.
          The press has no special right of access to
               prisons.
          A security problem is created.
          A public relations problem is created for the
               state.
          Televising executions is in poor taste.
          Televised executions would invade inmates'
               privacy.
          Televised executions would incite inmates.
          Televising executions would take the focus
               off the victims of crimes the condemned
               committed.

3.   The words suggest that print journalism is
limited in its ability to describe an execution, so
perhaps television should be permitted for the sake
of accurate reporting.

4.   Seville probably means that the public would
not appreciate the seriousness of the event and
would tune in to be entertained.

5. What is proper is hard to pin down; it
is often a function of taste, culture, and the
spirit of the times.

6. The conclusion, with its description of the
cyanide gas, harkens back to the introduction,
which also describes an execution.

Chapter Eleven   Remarkable People

p. 323   "Your Real Home Is Within"

1. Jones thought material things were important,
and he, therefore, feared that he would lose the
things he had acquired.

2. He probably means that for true happiness, we
must be sufficiently at peace with ourselves. That
is, contentment comes from within, not from
possessions.

3. Success and wealth do not guarantee happiness.

4. Many readers will say yes because Jones is a
man of remarkable talent who forged a career from
humble beginnings and fought his way back from both
physical and emotional illness.

5. Many readers will say yes because the mention
of Jones's name sparks some interest, and the
dramatic quotation is a grabber.

6. By comparing Jones to jazz greats Armstrong and
Parker, the conclusion emphasizes the importance of
Jones to American music.

p. 330   "Unforgettable Jane Edna Hill"

1. paragraphs 1-8: the growth of pampas flowers
for the Hill's wedding

paragraph 9: Jane Edna Hill is a literal gardener.

paragraphs 10, 15, 20, and 38: Jane as a figurative gardener, who "planted seeds of love"

paragraphs 47-48: Jane's legacy is a bigger garden with more gardeners to plant the "seeds of love."

2. He uses garden imagery because Jane Edna Hill's focal point for living was the biblical promise, "We plant the seed, but God makes it grow" (paragraph 6).

3. Responses will vary, but possibilities include:
     courageous
     loving
     unselfish
     religious
     giving
     kind
     strong
     faithful
     loyal

4. paragraphs 11-14; 15; 16-17; 19-20; 21-22; 23-33; 34

5. The examples give the reader insight into Jane Edna Hill's character because they are detailed, vivid illustrations of her behavior. In other words, the examples allow the author to show and not just tell.

6. Paragraphs 41-49 describe Jane Edna Hill's legacy and show that her life had such an impact that her "seeds of love" grow even after her death.

p. 337   "She Leads a Nation"

1. Like the Cherokees, Mankiller has brought herself back from a series of difficulties, showing great tenacity and courage. Also, more than once, like the Cherokees, she has had to start over.

2.   Many readers are likely to say yes because
Mankiller is the Chief of the Cherokee Nation of
Oklahoma; she has overcome poverty and illness, and
she has accomplished a great deal for her people.

3.   Mankiller was helped by her automobile accident and her
subsequent long, difficult recovery, which she got
through by relying on Cherokee precepts.

4.   Responses will vary, but these (among others)
are appropriate:

aggressive	caring
capable	dedicated
courageous	giving
strong	visionary
concerned	proud
hard-working	smart
respected	loved

5.   Responses will vary, but many readers may find
the last sentence dramatic and powerful because of
its brevity and simplicity, which contrasts with
the complexity of Mankiller's life.

6.   Responses will vary, but some readers may say
that they did not know about such things as the
Trail of Tears, relocating to urban slums, and lack
of self-determination.

p. 343   "Lee Atwater's Last Campaign"

1.   Atwater treated his cancer like the enemy--he
learned everything he could about it and plotted
the best course to defeat it, by striking at its
weakest point.

2.   In the conclusion, Atwater expresses that he
learned that people are the most important thing
in life, and human closeness is the sweetest thing
in life.

3.   Responses will vary, but many readers may feel
that his new-found religious orientation and
respect for people may have made it impossible for

44

him to keep the "killer instinct" of a successful
political figure.

4. Atwater probably wanted to share his
experiences and inform others of what he learned as
a result of his ordeal.

5. Many readers may find Atwater remarkable
because he fought his cancer bravely. He also
recognized and admitted his mistakes publicly and
shared the lessons he learned with those who read
his book.

p. 353 "You're Short, Besides"

1. Responses will vary, but many readers may say
that we do notice handicaps and what people cannot
do rather than what they can do.

2. A. Chan's father believed that his daughter
was paying for sins he had committed.

    B. Chan felt burdened because she had to try
to assuage her father's guilt.

3. Responses will vary.

4. She probably felt this way because she survived
the fall and the taunts, so she learned that such
things could not hurt her, and, therefore, they
need not be feared.

5. Responses will vary, but some readers may think
that when people ignore the handicapped, they may
be trying to be polite and not acknowledge a
problem. When they are patronizing, they may be
trying to be democratic and show that they believe
the handicapped are equal to others--that they can
dance.

6. Responses will vary, but some readers may find
the humor compatible with Chan's upbeat attitude.

7. Many readers will find Chan remarkable because
she never stopped trying to be as physically active

45

as she could be and because she accomplished a
great deal. Also, she has a positive attitude and,
as the conclusion shows, she has a sense of humor.

p. 360 Juliette Low: The Eccentric Who Founded
         The Girl Scouts"

1. Responses will vary, but many readers are
likely to say that the paragraph arouses interest
because it describes a person who arouses the
reader's curiosity because she seems so "counter-
culture."

2. A. She did "peculiar" things, like wear real
        vegetables in her hats.

        She felt women could do things that were
        traditionally not part of their role.

        She pulled stunts.

        She contested her husband's will.

        She was obstinant.

    B. Low would be much less eccentric by today's
standards.

3. Because she was so "eccentric," so outside the
norm, her birth on Halloween seems appropriate.

4. Low wanted the girls to be able to support
themselves without leaving home to work in the
factories.

5. Low felt women could assume any role, including
ones then denied to women. She also felt women
could have an education, a career, and a family.
In short, she saw women as strong, capable, and
worthy of self-determination.

6. Some readers may think that the title casts Low
in a negative light. Others may find it an

accurate preview of the essay's content and an accurate summation of Low's personality.

7.   Responses will vary, but many readers may find Low remarkable because she was independent in a time when it was difficult for women to be independent. She broke new ground, and in many ways was a visionary, making statements and performing deeds now commonplace as a result of the women's movement. Finally, Low's concern for others and willingness to take risks despite the personal cost are remarkable.

p. 368   "Mother Tongue"

1.   A.   Tan's mother felt limited, and knew that others perceived her as limited (para. 10).

     B.   Tan felt ashamed of her mother's English and felt her ideas were "imperfect " (para. 9).

          Tan would pretend to be her mother on the telephone (para. 10, Para. 14).

          Tan's academic possibilities were almost limited--she performed better in math and science than English and was steered by teachers toward math and science. (para. 15).

          Tan's writing style was influenced by her mother's speech (para. 21).

2.   Tan's mother knew that because of her limited English, people would not take her seriously.

3.   Tan believes that the "limited English" spoken in the home and teachers who steer students toward math and science explain why Asian Americans do better in math and science than in English.

4. Tan became a writer to disprove the assumption that writing was not her long suit.

5. Tan learned to envision an audience and to write clearly and simply.

6. A. Topic sentences appear in paragraphs 2, 3, 4, 5, 7, 8, 9, 10, 14, 15, 16, 17, 18, 19, 20, and 21.

    B. The topic sentences provide landmarks that guide the reader so he or she is always clear about a paragraph's focus.

Chapter Twelve   Current Issues

p. 375 "Big White"

1. The sentences flow well because there is a variety of sentence openers in the first two paragraphs.

2. A. Responses will vary.

    B. Specific yet simple word choice contributes to the effective description.

3. Rozin's frustration was enormous because he thought he had devised the perfect plan to best the machine and get what he wanted, but the machine found a new way of thwarting him.

4. Rozin is probably serious about the fact that machines frustrate us, but his tongue is firmly in his cheek for any statement stronger than that.

5. All the responses are possible. The good vs. evil theme becomes apparent when Rozin calls the

machine "White Devil." The control vs.
helplessness theme is seen because Rozin loses
control, but the machine doesn't. And the human
vs. machine theme is the primary thrust of the
narrative.

6. The machine has won; the essay ends with
personification because like a human, the machine
is capable of taunting.

p. 379 "Drinking: A Problem for Our Society"

1. Many readers will find that the introduction
stimulates their interest. The description of the
party animal engages interest; the shirt slogan is
amusing to some; the irony of "he's got a problem"
is engaging.

2. paragraph 7: The drinking behavior of adults
    runs counter to behavior we tell our children
    to exhibit.

    paragraph 9: The father of the suspended
    quarterback sued the school board.

    paragraph 11: Children think that being adult
    means drinking.

    paragraph 12: A motorman's drinking killed 5
    in New York.

    paragraph 13: Rape charges against William
    Kennedy Smith included accounts of drinking.

    paragraph 14: The prosecutor says that alcohol
    is a factor in most crimes.

3. Adults encourage young people to drink
primarily by example (paragraph 7) and by not
abiding by the rules (paragraph 9).

4. In our culture, no one likes a "squealer," and
people hesitate to get involved.

5. something like: We don't know how to handle alcohol (paragraph 6), which leads to contradictory views about it (paragraph 16). However, what we should do is publicly disapprove of it (paragraph 17).

6. Quindlen closes with a position statement (one that forms part of the thesis). Some readers may find the conclusion boring.

p. 384 "Taking the Test"

1. Responses will vary, but one likely reason is that by sharing his experience, Groff can help others understand something of the fear homosexuals live with. His essay can, therefore, inform the reader and earn the reader's compassion for homosexuals.

2. Groff uses the capital letter to emphasize the importance the test has.

3. A. blood on the subway: a reminder of the fear and public disgust associated with AIDS

   B. the click of the refrigerator door: perhaps the finality--the closure-- associated with the test results

   C. the woman in black: a reminder that AIDS victims are not just gay males

   D. First Avenue and the bad art: a reminder that people whose lives are threatened find beauty where they didn't see it before

   E. the pores of the doctor's face: perhaps a reminder that people whose lives are threatened look more closely

4. If Groff shared the results of this test, the reader's suspense would be relieved, and some of

50

the essay's power would be lost. The reader would
perhaps be grateful for the happy ending or perhaps
conclude that only gay males get AIDS so there is
less to worry about.

5. Responses will vary, but one possibility is
that life is uncertain for all of us--AIDS is just
one reason for that--so we should experience and
savor as much as we can while we are able to.

6. Responses will vary.

p. 391 "Be Scared for Your Kids"

1. something like: Drugs kill.

2. Paragraph 11 indicates that he did not think it
was dangerous.

3. In paragraphs 7 and 25, Sicherman notes that he
blames himself for not warning his son about the
dangers of LSD.

4. Responses will vary, but one likely meaning is
that all living things die and pass into an unknown
state.

5. A. A likely audience is parents and children.

    B. A likely purpose is to convince parents to
warn their children off drugs and to convince
children not to take drugs.

6. Responses will vary.

p. 396 "A Crime of Compassion"

1. The title reflects the irony and contradiction
inherent in our ability and obligation to prolong
life when an individual no longer wants to live.

2. something like: We need laws giving terminally ill patients the right to die.

3. The description of the macho cop provides a powerful contrast to what Mac became in six months. This contrast provides a dramatic statement of the ravages of cancer and, therefore, the need for the "crime of compassion."

4. Huttmann moves the reader's emotions and earns sympathy with vivid descriptions of Mac's suffering and its toll on the family.

5. The quotations show that Mac and his wife favored the mercy-killing. Thus, they lend force to Huttmann's argument. They also add to the poignancy of the piece.

6. A. The legal alternative is that the doctor could write a no-code order.

    B. It is contradictory and hypocritical that the doctor can permit mercy-killing, but the nurse cannot.

p. 401 "The Ways of Meeting Oppression"

1. acquiescence--evil and taken as proof of blacks'
                   inferiority

    violence--impractical and immoral

    nonviolent resistance--makes it possible for
                   blacks to stay in the South and
                   enlists all good people in the
                   struggle for equality

2. This may be because people fear the unknown and often would rather maintain the status quo--no matter how unpleasant--than risk uncertainty.

3. A. paragraphs 1 and 2

   B. The examples help clarify King's
generalizations.

4. A. paragraphs 3, 5, 6, 7, 9, and 10

   B. The cause and effect analysis in paragraphs
3, 5, and 6 explains what happens when people
accept their oppression passively or when they
react violently. These examples clarify why
resignation and violence are not acceptable
responses to oppression. In paragraphs 7, 9, and
10, the cause and effect analysis shows the
positive results of nonviolent resistance to
establish that this kind of resistance is the
superior response to oppression.

5. Responses will vary, but many readers may feel
they would better understand what nonviolent
resistance is if an example or two were provided.

6. Blacks are referred to as Negroes.

   The language excludes women. (For example,
     in paragraph 3: "Religion reminds every
     man that he is his brother's keeper.")

7. King probably means that nonviolence allows
people to support the principles of justice,
regardless of their race.

p. 408 "Invasion of the Body Snatchers: Fetal
         Rights vs. Mothers' Rights"

1. A. Paragraphs 1-4 seem to support court-
ordered cesarean sections, particularly because
paragraph 2 is so dramatic and paragraph 4
indicates that even the mother favored the courts
making the decision.

53

B.   Paragraphs 5 and 6 are a surprise because
they go in the opposite direction, indicating that
court-ordered cesarean sections should be opposed.

2.   We now possess the ability to intervene
medically to assist a fetus when we did not in the
past.

3.   for
     The legislation would help prevent the birth
     of deformed, retarded, and addicted babies
     that are a burden on society.

     When a mother chooses to have a baby, she
     should abide by certain standards.

     against
     The fetus's location in the mother makes it
     impossible for it to have rights.

     The interest of the fetus can be in conflict
     with the interest of the mother.

     The laws would be used against poor and
     minority women who don't get adequate
     prenatal care.

     Procedures like cesarean sections just
     generate money for doctors.

     The mothers often make the right decision.

     Medical decisions are merely a matter of
     playing the odds.

4.   Responses will vary, but some readers may argue
that enough women hurt fetuses to make fetal
protection legislation a good idea.

5.   A.   The first example serves as support for
court-ordered cesarean sections, and the second
example supports letting the mother decide.

     B.   The example in paragraph 21 helps prove
that medical science is not always correct in its
decisions.

6. Sandroff opposes legislation and court-ordered procedures to protect the fetus. The first clue is the title. The next indication is paragraph 7, sentence 1. Finally, paragraphs 30 and 31 clearly present her view on the issue.

- NOTES -

- NOTES -

- NOTES -

- NOTES -